RHYTHM OF BENJAMIN

WHEN ALEC IS LOVE !

AVINASH KUMAR SINGH

THIS BOOK IS PROUDLY DEDICATED TO ALEC BENJAMIN AND HIS LOVELY FANS . I HOPE YOU WILL LOVE TO READ ALEC FROM MY POINT OF VIEW.

Contents

Contents

Acknowledgements

Alec Benjamin is an American singer and songwriter . Every people who are fond of him take their major perspective to fall in love with his creations . He have such a unique voice , very good at lyrics and the most favourite one , the storytelling . Though I'm an Indian ,I don't discover American artists much . Bollywood is in trend here and we get to listen the English songs just for chill or hook. When I heard Alec most popular track "let me down slowly" for the first time , I never expected that songs like this can exist in current era . To explore Alec with my certainty and conclusive facts , I wrote this book – Rhythm of Benjamin . His every song hits me too hard and I caught myself trapped in his words dimensions very soon .

This book has 20 songs poem which are almost with same sense of Alec's two albums – Narrated for you and These two windows . Hope you can connect with the words here too.

Thank you ! ☺

Prologue

Alec Benjamin talks about devil , mind and heart emotions . He conveys very dark meaning with his songs . His Narrated for you Album was a blockbuster in the industry just because of one song 'let me down slowly' . Every one know in better way that this guy deserve millions of support and love from natives . He will touch this number soon .

This book is just a start of my life with Alec . I know he's unaware about me and my business. Avinash , welcome you all in this journey .

See you at the end ! Happy reading .

About The Author

Avinash Kumar Singh is an Indian love writer . He usually writes about nature and human love . He released his two books – Kinda love (It hurts when it's true) and 28 pixels of February (poetries bleeds ink) . He's 17 and a romantic writer of modern era . He don't link grammar with the literature . He wants to create his own world of literature where people feel about the each word with the phase of different stanzas.

Avinash's mind has a unique space for James Allen and heart for William Wordsworth . His dream is to achieve success in his writing and write best seling books so far.

About The Singer

Alec Benjamin was born on 28 May 1994 . He is an American songwriter who is master of his lyrics and storytelling. Alec gained popularity with his songs demons and ruled over millions of heart with his track let me down slowly (from Narrated for you).

Currently he has released his 3 albums successfully –

- NARRATED FOR YOU
- THESE TWO WINDOWS
- UNCOMMENTARY

His These two windows album was the most emotional album and for the same reason every Benjamin can relate it to their life with ease. Read these poems to catch special meaning of those songs in just few lines . Don't forget to listen them too.

narrated for you

The album was released in year 2018 and was first Album from Alec Benjamin . Almost every song in this album was narrated for someone who was very close to Alec's heart.

• If we have each other

• Water fountain

• Annabelle's homework

• Let me down slowly

• Swim

• Boy in the bubble

• Steve

• Gotta be a reason

• If I killed someone for you

• Death of a hero

1. if we have each other

I got you girl,
You can't hide from me anymore .
I heard your cry,
It's different, varies from before.
You got something tripping and crazy ,
You can't feel alone in this night.
I know it's not easy ,
feeling alright.
Girl don't fear from dark spirits,
Believe me if we have each other;
Nothing else will bother .
We can escape every tragedy .
This world is fine ,
not so worse,
If we have each other ,
we're free from each curse.

2. water fountain

She told me that she love me by water fountain
I don't see her now from year since ten.
She's lost in herself somewhere , I remember .
I waited for her from decade of December.
Where is she now ?
I mean did she left
But she promised me ,
that she will meet me by water fountain.
I feel like she is busy with something else
Something that matter more than fountain base .
Now I realise that that the promise was young
The water is now dried and the love she dumped.

3. annabelle's homework

She handled me her notebook .
I can't ignore her innocent look .
She says she is busy with some work .
So I moved calmly to school nook.
I open her note and the front page
Her name was embedded with my ink.
I again made a overwriting,
Found my expectations and reality fighting.
I spent 22 days and 21 nights
Make her notes look alright.
She doesn't even praise my efforts
Yet I feel so calm with her happy face ,
Doesn't think much about whatever I write.

4. let me down slowly

This night is yours and mine
To the morning from this nine .
You can't make me unhappy now
We should stay together anyhow .
You can't get off the fact you said
You can't weep for the love ; no regrets
I want to spend my life with you
So please , please
Could you find a way to let me down slowly
I hope you should think about this calmly
Doesn't matter anything more than this ,
Just I want you to stay very truly .
Please raise me up
Wake me up
I'm fighting with the bad dreams
Please wave me up
Live me up
I'm shouting with loud screams .
So please , please Could you find a way to let me down slowly
I hope you should think about this calmly
Doesn't matter anything more than this ,
Just I want you to stay very truly.

5. swim

I've been drowning so deep,
Feeling hard to breathe for now.
I can't see any dry land so far .
I need you with no cause .
Another 40 days I'm lost at sea
I'm just gonna swim until you love me .
Hoping everything will turn okay soon.
Not under sun but maybe under moon.
I'm feeling so alone
Save me with your presence
I want to hit your heart so hard
with bunches of our love essence.

6. boy in the bubble

It was early in the morning
On my way to home .
Few feets later
I was caught alone .
My mom caught me in black and blue
She said why you're changing through .
I got no regrets on the caught
Cause for my imperfections I had to fought.
Punch my face , Do it cause I like the pain
Everything is not about the grace
You want the satisfaction for your gain .

7. steve

Once there was a boy
Called Steve by the all
He knows about the world
About the rise and the fall
He got to know about the fact
Of the taste of the fruits
Of the hidden lies
And the factual truths.

8. gotta be a reason

There's always a reason
Behind your presence
Presence in the world
To fill each absence.
You're special for something
Or something turn you specified
Like your life without emotions
Turns everything complicated and terrified.
There's a gotta be a reason you're earth
Look for the goal and secret of your birth.

9. if i killed someone for you

Drowning in the red
With blood on my hand
I got no escape.
Not it's not any theft .
I did a mistake
Not a mistake but a crime
I ran through the woods
But nothing seems to be fine
Rinsing of my clothes
I mean to come to you
Please help me my love
I'm about to loose .
No don't deny to save me
Cause I killed someone for you .
The one I killed is me
I changed for you fine decently
No I got no turning back.
I'm facing my strength as my lacks .
Please hide me in your home
I'm feeling all alone .
Please help me to turn in you .
Cause I killed someone for you.

10. death of a hero

Death of a hero
Is a miserable fact
Innovation of a zero
A faithful impact.
I'm drowning in the tears
I'm turning slow and defined.
My love is in my tears
And death is already signed .
There's death of a hero .
Death of a legend
Death of a hero
Got everything in it's blend

these two windows

These two windows was released in year 2020. When everyone was strugling to live their decent life , Alec imposed his hard work and passion heavily on the situation .

This album has most emotional and connecting songs which can make a sensitive heart to cry soon . This is my fav album too. I hope you will love this part of book more enough .

- Mind is a prison
- Demons
- Oh my god
- The book of you and I
- Match in the rain
- Jesus in LA
- I'm not a cynic
- Alamo
- Must have been the wind
- Just like you

11. mind is a prison

My mind doesn't seems perfect
it loads my soul and control.
It's a prison of no escape
the love between us ends in a troll.
I live inside my circle
my mind resides me in it .
I don't know cause of this trap
it conveys the convention of givin'
My mind is a prison
and I'm never gonna get out
Maybe it's targetting a mission
to capture my in and out .

12. demons

I have got these demons
hiding at a distance.
These demons explains
feelings of absence .
I got to know these each and all
demons are dark ,
and dark sometimes fall.
I have got these demons
failing to reach the fall of absence .

13. oh my god

Oh my god these are the words
words of my poetry.
Senseless for many around,
limited for someone surround.
Oh my god look at these skies
give us motivation to fly so high.
also the fear of falling so bad.
scrambled words that make you mad .
Oh my god this is unexpected
you are done adjusted.

14. the book of you and i

Look at these pages Alec
look at this book of you and I
Alec , read these words
for you and from my
my heart which hold your smile.
you travel in mind
in nerves for several mile .
I don't know how to peek in you
my love that passes through .
My mind is a escape
a way to your dimension
A dream is to meet you love
a goal of profound creation.

15. match in the rain

I fought for her so hard
in the days and the dark.
I want to confess my each for her
the each that matters ;
without a perfect imperfection.
not in wavy rain.
Please look in my eyes
don't make me feel like this
like I'm trying to light a match in the rain.

16. jesus in la

He's not immortal .
He will die one day , will cry one day .
when you lost your slumber
that in memory of crying way .
your'e terrified for your paths
and you won't find jesus in la.
nothing feels like a okay
and rests will act perfectly determined
cause you won't find jesus in la .

17. i'm not a cynic

I'm being optimistic , like nobody before
I'm being sarcastic but no one calls me more .
but wait what is this
belive my fate and me.
like the see of coming,
everyone in we.
I'm not a cynic
but today's not my day.
make a angle of 360 ways.
I'm wrong but not a cynic,
belive me and my faith in it.

18. alamo

Let's count our problems
let's hear the sound of our make
let's belive the summer and the warmth
Let's spot the cherry of your cake .
It's tendemous ,
quite false for now .
you can't imaginate the pixels
like all these alamo on the ground.
throw your pieces of context ,
throw the rest on the wound .
It's true to say about dust,
like all these alamo on the ground .

19. must have been the wind

I heard a shattering from the apartment above mine,
A glass into multiple pieces cracked so fine .
I thought this was a dream,
but then I heard the cry of girl in the same line .
I ran through stairs ,
walked down the hall;
knocked upon her door
maybe she ignored my call.
I punched the patience
soon she came out.
asked me for what I'm here,
I asked things I heard so loud .
She said - i think your ear playing tricks on you .
There's nothing like this happened now .
maybe it's a noise of a wind .
Though thanks for reaching me anyhow.

20. just like you

I fought a lot,
with my dad, like a nonsense.
I blocked his call,
thought he controls my sense .
I feel shame for this all,
my father hold our family so strong .
He saved us in pandemic from fall ;
realised how I was so wrong .
Your'e the best dad,
You understand me too .
one day i'll have son or daughter ,
I hope I will be just ike you.

Thank You

HOPE YOU LOVED THE BOOK FOR YOUR REVIEWS -

INSTAGRAM - phenomenal.curves

DO FOLLLOW

ALEC BENJAMIN SUPPORT HIM VERY MUCH .

THANKS FOR READING GUYS !

9 798887 172354

Printed by Libri Plureos GmbH in Hamburg,
Germany